ECHOES OF SILENCE
Poems
by
Helen Hayes Veitch

Helen Hayes Veitch

Published by

Hope Spring Publishers
P. O. Box 9343
Bolton, Connecticut 06043

Printed in The United States of America

To Maria

With thanks for sharing with me
a friendship truly in the Spirit of God.

My sincere thanks

To my dear husband Jim for his love and support throughout the years.

To Rev. Robert Cronin for his guidance and friendship. To Rev. Oliver Renaud, O.M.I., my Spiritual Director, for his patience, insights and knowledge shared. To my friend Patricia Myette for proofreading the manuscript, and for her many helpful suggestions. To Ruth Ladd, Mary Joan MacArthur, and Joan Gordon for their encouragement and suggestions, and to Donna Boylan for her help with anything and everything. To my friend Maria Decsy for sharing so many thoughts of God, and the Spiritual Journey with me — Many of our conversations led to poems.

Poetry is a gateway to prayer. It draws and silences the heart, it empties it to a point where one is turned inside out and ends up on the other side of silence — which is none other than the heart of God.

Read each poem with reverence, with awe and with openness. Let it silence your heart, let it draw you into its milieu. They fell from the heart of God into the mind, heart and hands of Helen — Let the Creator's words now go back to him together with your heart and being, and let it accomplish what it was sent to do.

Maria Deasy

Bolton, Ct.
April 17, 1988

I SEEK YOU

I seek You frantically without.
In frenzied search I dash about,
To seek in words for just one clue,
To help me find my way to You.
My feelings tell me You are there,
But urgency distracts me. "Where?"
And worldly as I've grown to be,
I lose the moment You touch me.
Resuming searching, longing, seeking,
I grasp at words another's speaking.
I anxiously evaluate.
In reasoning, again I'm late.
The whispered, patient words within,
Are lost again in frenzied din.
And now, in feigned humility,
I mock another's way to Thee:
In words arranged in every way,
By others seeking what You say.
Persistently, You speak to me,
And then Your Grace enlightens me.
Why seek You in another's mind
For answers, when within I find
The Source of all we can possess,
In stillness waiting to express,
In simple terms, for me alone,
The seeds of Love, that You have sown.

March 4, 1982

1

YEARNING

My heart is open unto Thee.
My mind invokes a silent plea.
My troubled soul implicitly
Expresses my temerity.

The pulsing of internal quest,
Evokes need for the Divine Guest.
My faltering, fumbling, prayers express,
My wavering faith and hopelessness.

Foolhardy as I seem to be,
My yearning draws me close to Thee,
And nearness magnifies the pain
Of fruitless searching; little gain.

But You Who know my inner stress,
Make known the path to happiness.
In ways that mystify and thrill,
And Grace that reinforces will.

And through the hope of Saving Grace,
Repentance cleanses inner space,
Preparing for the Guest Supreme,
Fulfilling hope, and faith, and dream.

March 21, 1982

FOLLOWING CHRIST

It's a heavy Cross that you must bear,
The Cross of Christ, you chose to share.
It hobbled Christ. You'll falter too,
But the Risen Christ will be with you.

Christ suffered pain. You'll suffer too.
But the Healing Christ will comfort you.
Christ fell, oppressed by mankind's sin.
You too may fall, but rise in Him.

Christ's friends deserted Him when tried.
When tested, friends may leave your side.
But for every heartache that you bear,
The joy of Christ's loyal love you'll share.

Christ's action earned the right to win
The way to God, and conquer sin.
By yours, you'll teach, and touch, and guide
Those needing help to reach His side.

You may be tempted to despair,
Or pride may prove a devil's snare,
But guided by the Spirit's light,
Your will can turn your deeds aright.

In serving Him, Who serves us all,
You're answering His Father's call.
And through His Grace, His Spirit will raise
Your soul on high, to serve and praise.

March 26, 1982

THE DEVIL

The devil with his devious ways,
Confuses me at times and plays
Upon my tender conscience — (Pride?)
To lead me to the other side.

My muddled mind mistakenly
Makes good seem wrong, and sin agree
With virtue's goals, and right's success,
And makes all choices just a guess.

To strive towards goals so well obscured
Seems foolish, when the "NOW'S" assured,
With visions of the pleasures "NOW"
So clear compared to future's "HOW?"

I'm subject to the devil's ploy,
When weakness makes me evil's toy.
But Grace could lead me back again,
If I could choose with acumen.

For habit towards the righteous way
Defeats temptation's feet of clay,
To take the "NOW" and "HOW?" in stride,
Accepting God's way, though implied.

April 21, 1982

ENTER SPIRIT

God's Spirit enters through the heart.
You feel it's being torn apart,
To wrest away the pride and sin,
Now eating at it from within.

The anguish steals inside your soul,
And makes each question take its toll
In tears and pain and mental stress,
'Till all you feel is helplessness.

The pain will be replaced with longing,
And a fearful sense of not belonging.
And then your motives will be tested —
Your life, your present, your past, divested.

Demons waiting to entrap you.
Evil thoughts strive to enwrap you.
In frustration, turn to pleasure.
Seek out joy in earthly treasure.

With a sense of deep confusion,
You discover false illusions,
And grasp at momentary snatches
Of hope your anxious searching catches.

At times a respite will refresh you,
But again the torment will possess you.
To conquer it, you must embrace it.
Then your will resolves to face it.

You feel you know not what you're seeking,
And doubt the very words you're speaking.
To help you cope, you seek distraction.
The Spirit responds with firmer action.

(Continued)

Though the pain seems past enduring:
Thoughts of God's Grace are assuring.
Then His Fire will burn within you,
And your anguish will continue.

Then in trembling, fear, and fright,
You seek refuge now, in flight.
Though you flee, you can't escape it.
Pursued with love, you can't evade it.

The frantic feeling, now will haunt you.
The deft pursuit of Spirit will taunt you.
And then in utter desperation,
You admonish God for your creation.

Now repentance makes its way.
Willingly the price, you'll pay.
'Tis then The Spirit takes possession,
Knowing now, you've learned the lesson.

Now, you're utterly defeated.
Now, with all your strength depleted.
Remorse and sorrow overtake you.
Now in guilt, will God forsake you?

Silence, waiting, anguish, yearning,
Tearful, anxious, tortured, fearing,
Now a space within you clearing.
Now can enter strength for bearing.

Spirit's Wisdom seeps in soothing.
Pain-filled passions gently smoothing.
Promises of joy-filled moments,
Tenderly replace the torments.

(Continued)

Though trials that come seem past endurance,
With His Spirit's deft assurance
That with Faith comes strength to bear,
And Christ's Love, with Grace to share.

Peace may last but for the moment,
But with promised help, the torments
Hold, but little threat to smite you,
Now with Spirit's Grace to right you.

In the Cross of Christ you're sharing.
Through the Spirit's strength you're bearing,
And through Wisdom's light uniting
You to Christ's loyal love, requiting.

May 14, 1982

SPIRIT

Spirit, stay with me awhile.
Lift my spirit, *"Spirit* style."
Spirit out the voice of gloom.
Dispel the harbingers of doom.
While I struggle, counsel me.
Understanding, set me free.
Spirit's fire warm my soul.
Demonstrate benign control.
Treat me mildly, tenderly.
Show to me, *Love's* charity.
Spirit up my faith in Thee.
Swell my soul with piety.
With Your Gifts' and Fruits' delights
Spirit me to *Spirit*ual heights.

June 24, 1982

PRESENCE

How marvelous it is to be
Created to Your imagery:
With Spirit harbored deep inside
The body-temple, there to bide.
An intellect to light the way,
Reflecting Spirit inspired rays,
To guide me through the perilous haze,
Or blinding glare that faults my gaze.
And yet, unseeing, I can know
Your presence, by the inner glow:
And feelings, strangely so intense
That they awaken every sense;
And surge through heart and soul and mind
To more intensify the Find.
'Til mortal vessel containing that Wealth,
Contracts to exorcise the self,
And writhing there 'twixt joy and pain,
There's naught but Love that can remain.
And love responds to Love to be,
Alive, not I, but You in me.
And then, as if suspended there,
I am not self, but offered fare,
And in the presence, Lord, of Thee,
Have no desire, other, to be.

July 28, 1982

ALONE

I am alone. No one can share
The fear and anguish, doubt, despair
That reaches deep within my soul,
While You suppress the earthly hold.
No one can bear the pain with me,
Or clear my view, that I might see
Or guide my faltering steps, in flight
'Til You, Oh Spirit, share Your light.
I can reach out and grasp and strain
And then, in fear, draw back again
Unsure of vision, path, or goal
Or calm, to ease my suffering soul.
I call on strength, unleashed by God,
To plod towards goals unknown, untrod
To seek a Lover beckoning
With painful questions — Promising
Me taunts and trials and anguished cries
To follow unto death. The logic of the
    world belies
The breath of love, in whispers wrought
With fleeting answers, deftly caught
And held in hope, and then despair,
For worldly lures dispel it there.
Buoyed up, by tender spiritual lifts,
On wings of love — The Spirit's gift.
Again spurred on to grief, unknown,
Except by One, Who walked alone,
And bore the suffering, grief, and pain,
Of all who followed, to leave again.
No one did share His pain — Our shame.
His way did bear no thought of blame.

(Continued)

Accepting, knowing God, His will,
Went unto death. His love-heart stilled.
But not for long, constrained by death,
He rose again. He'd paid our debt.
He knows the pain. He knows the price.
He knows the path. He knows the choice.
I'll follow Him, His will, His time,
His painful path — His way, not mine.
He, Who in my unworthy soul,
Resides when'er my will can hold
The evil strands of life at bay,
For He alone can lead the way.
His Spirit speaks in silent sounds,
To ears attuned — thoughts so profound,
Unheard by others, though so near,
The satiate strains of love, so dear,
To quell the loneliness of one,
Who seeks the company of His Son.

September, 1982

MY WILL IS YOURS

I am not self — My will is Yours.
As long as mortal life endures
I have no strength,
Except in You.
You make the choice
I'll follow through.
I have no voice in what I do.
I've given over all to You.

You are my strength
You are my voice
You are my mind
Yours is the choice
I can not choose to turn away.
The final choice, I made today.
With all the will You gave to me,
I will to give my will to Thee.

'Though I have known
This was the way,
I feared the price
I'd have to pay.
You've left me nothing else to do,
Except to offer me to You.
My life is Yours — Do what You will.
An empty vessel — Yours to fill.

November 5, 1982

BEACON

A steadfast beacon summons me,
And anxiously I seek the place.
By signs familiar, yet unknown,
I'm drawn to dwell within the space.
As leaves are driven by the breeze,
And placed where e'er the wind might will,
The soul within is stirred,
And wafted up and then is stilled.
Then touched. Enchanting gifts proffered.
Then bathed in warming, spiritual light
And tossed on buoyant waves of love,
And lifted to undreamed of heights
To drift through haze of dream-like clouds,
Then wash upon the tranquil shore,
And soothed, and left in sweet repose,
To wait, and just adore.

November 12, 1982

NATURE

How beauty doth escape my try,
When in presumption, I imply
That with my paper, paint, and brush,
I could capture nature's blush.
I vainly try to imitate
The marvelous world that You create.
Its elegance excites my soul
With living warmth and depth of cold.
I close my eyes, and I can see
Your beauties still possessed in me,
Through Your created sight and sense
And feelings made the more intense
By knowing, surely, You are there
Reflected by Your loving care
Of plant and flower, and sky, and tree,
And boundless life surrounding me.
In steps I take, I feel the spring
Of nature's living carpeting.
The visions are so limitless
That they're impossible to express.
For there remains not time to see
The beauties within reach of me.
But humbly I'm compelled to try
To capture touch of earth and sky,
That my attempts may clearly show,
God, I admire Your Creations so.

1982

PATIENT LOVE

You keep the universe in place
Created it from empty space
Can reach me — touch my very soul,
And yet, I think *I'm* in control.

You guide the moon, and sun around,
And hold the world within its bounds.
You even stem the stormy sea,
And yet, you still find time for me.

The magnitude of living things
Confounds the mind, and often brings
Me to the point of awe, and fear —
"To be so wondrous, yet so near!"

My doubts are not what you deserve.
And less, my faltering tries to serve,
And yet, You seem to value me.
How patient Your great love can be!

If love like Yours can but endure
This foolish fledgling — so unsure,
My efforts, while so weak and dim,
May someday grow through Life within.

January 31, 1983

LOVE

No other love is so sublime.
No other can so quicken mine.
No other can such promise give.
No other offer Grace to live.
Its scope can reach a distant place.
Its strength can conquer wall or space.
It touches deep within the soul
And draws you out, and makes you whole.
And lovingly, Love comforts you.
And lovingly, Love waits for you.
And lovingly, Love leads the way.
And though you fall, unyielding stays.
With tenderness, Love's ways entice.
And yet, though gift, demands a price.
Will self-love, from Love, bar the way?
Is "all" too great a price to pay?
Can you abandon all but Love?
With whole abandon love but Love?
Love may cost all, but Love's rewards
Await the one who loves the Lord.

April 20, 1983

EASTER HOPE

The barren branches, bowed and bent,
Have borne the burden of winter, spent.
And newly fallen, late spring snow
Weighs heavily on fir tree boughs.
The hollow of the meadow holds
A hidden message in its folds.
Surrounding trees, their bark still bare,
Accent the sharpness of the air.
The sepulcher-like, ice bound pond
Reflects the morbid scene around.
But growing circles catch the light,
Awakening sense of sound and sight.
The croaking frogs, their message send
Of life triumphant — Winter's end.
Then, as if keyed to Easter's hope,
The whole bleak picture, in a stroke
Of living sound, awakening,
Proclaims our resurrected King.

May 6, 1983

THE MAKER'S HAND

The waves approach the dry, parched shore,
And lap the sand, and gently pour
Life through small rivulets in the sand,
To stir, and move, as if unplanned.
They seep into each thirsting pore
Impulsive, splashing, reach towards more.
Then thrill by bursts of warmth and cold,
To firmly pack the trembling shoal.
And slowly then, the tide line creeps
Still farther up, until it peaks
And touches every sandy grain,
And comes and goes, and thrills again.
Each moment brings a new surprise,
Each tingling grain awaits the rise
And fall of tidal wash in fear —
For will that blithe, engulfing tear
Entrap it, to be swept alone,
Into the Ocean's dark unknown?
But then, time slowly breaks the spell,
And starts the fall, known but too well.
For solace such as this must end,
And then the shore accepts, and spends
The time just waiting 'till the tides
Return — Cooled from the deeper side.
But suddenly, a force unknown
Propells the cleansing, love kissed foam
To rise again to greater heights
And then, each grain of sand delights
In thrills, more precious for promised wane,
And bathes the grains in tender pain.
Oh, will it leave? Oh, will it stay?

(Continued)

Oh, Heaven has such startling ways
Of reaching, touching, tortuous love,
And powered by forces from above,
There's nothing known that can dispel
The strong and surging, smothering, swell
Of loving force, that laps and strokes
The thirsting shore, and sweetly soaks
Each parched and longing grain of sand.
"All guided by The Maker's Hand."

June 15, 1983

WITHIN

I lose my way while seeking You,
Among the pleasures I pursue
So avidly; then but to grasp
A thread of joy; naught but a gasp
Of life — Much less
Than that true life I now possess.
Within!

I wander through familiar things.
The sight of worldly treasures bring
Me nothing but a fleeting view
Compared to what I have with You.
And yet, so worldly I have grown,
I keep pursuing what I've known.
Without!

I've but to open up my mind
To know Your will, and then I'll find
My way, amid the false milieu,
And recognize that if I do,
What that true light dictates to me —
I'll find no greater wealth then Thee.
Within!

July, 1983

THE LOVING PRESENCE

I live in the presence of a Loving Presence,
and yet I remain unaware of It.
If, in Its goodness, It touches me with
awareness, even momentarily, I withdraw
from It, because to recognize
The Presence, I would have to recognize
my unworthiness.
Throughout the years, my life has been a
see-saw battle within myself, of need
for this Presence, and reaching towards It,
and fearful withdrawal, lest It demand
more of me than I am willing to give.
In compromise, I give limited amounts of
myself — gifts, talents, a little love
(If "love" is truly love when it is limited)
Only enough to ease a world-wise
conscience —
Only enough to allow me to be free to
close the door to openness and
unlimited love.
With every closing door, the weakness
strengthens the evil and the good in me
is diminished.
Fear of the Loving Presence becomes greater,
because the attraction of the world
takes on a brighter glow in the sight of
half-closed eyes — Eyes that close to
shelter themselves from the luminous light
of The Loving Presence.
In need, time and again, I turn to
The Loving Presence,

(Continued)

27

Recognizing the Presence through
  Its Light of Grace, but retreating from It
  when the time of need is past,
Because reason tells me that such a Presence
  demands a response — Demands more
  response than I am ready to give.
In the belief that the all-merciful Presence
  will understand my weakness, even my
  faults, I live out life in a pattern of
  giving only what is minimally demanded,
  taking from the world whatever was the
  world's to give, within the limits I believe
  to be acceptable; Accepting from The
  Loving Presence, all that It is willing
  to give. . .
Willingly gambling that there will be time
  at the end of life, or in a purgatory
  thereafter, to give whatever is necessary
  to gain The Loving Presence for all
  eternity. . .
An unknown eternity, compared to the
  worldly known, and in my fear
  I remain apart.
Repeatedly, I draw upon the Love of
  The Loving Presence
Not even recognizing the Great Love
  because earthly estimations of love
  obscure It.
Its limitlessness is constantly limited by
  my limits. . .
My unwillingness to give of myself, and
  my God-given love —
My reluctance to give makes of my love a

(Continued)

lifeless imitation of what God meant it to be,
and diminishes my life and the
opportunities to recognize
The Loving Presence accordingly.
But The Loving Presence is a persistent Love.
It is a Love sacrificial unto death;
    A death of anguish;
A death on the Cross.
The warmth of this love penetrates the
    coldness of self-love and permeates the
    shell-like wall of time.
This love need not penetrate from without
    because The Loving Presence is within me.
In the pause of worldly activity; In the words
    of a friend;
In the words of Holy Scripture; The way is
    opened by simple openness.
The Presence is felt and known.
In the knowledge of The Loving Presence,
    barriers, years in the making, melt away
    — cease to exist.
In the strengthening presence of that Love,
    I am enabled to look at the evil and face it;
    And with the help of The Loving Presence
    break the barriers. With persistence,
    born of Grace, I can rebuild the fallen
    structure of the Temple of God which I am,
    and rise in praise of The Loving Presence.

September 5, 1983

BE

I'll follow Lord; You lead the way.
I'll try to learn to wait and pray;
Not "Do" nor "Undo" what You've done.
Be patient! Learn that You're the One
Who acts: I must but "Be" for You.
Not even question what You do.
I've thought, so long, I was the one
To do the deeds that must be done.
But through Your Grace, I shall await
Your action and maintain a state
Of watchful love, until I hear
Love's silent sounds so sweet and clear,
To signal that You're present now
Within my soul, to show me how
To "Be," and You will make of me
Whatever I am meant to be.

December 16, 1983

QUESTIONING

What place is this, where we exist
The fear and anguish, pain, and risks,
That make of us tormented shells
Enclosed within a man-made hell?

The painful barbs and hurtful speech
Of those we love and those we reach
To help, leave our souls with
   wounds and scars
Our spirits imprisoned by vengeful bars

Our loving acts returned as strikes
Our loving words as piercing spikes
Our loving thoughts as fruitless vines
Seem snarled and trapped as hate entwines

'Tis all a waste — To love, To share
'Tis futile to reach out or care
Why reach towards love, when love escapes?
Why not grasp life? He wins, who takes

But vision stretched beyond my reach
Invites — No calls — Commands me! —
   Seek
The way of Love that Christ made plain
Regardless of the strife or pain

Through God, as man, our way was paved
Our Souls by sacrifice He saved
His light will set our spirits free
His love our source of strength will be.

(Continued)

And then, as soft as falling snow,
I'll feel His touch, and love will grow
and spread, until my heart may burst
"It's You, alone, for Whom I thirst!"

And I will face the barbs and pain
A thousand times, if You remain
And I can know Your Love and You
No threat is worse than losing You.

1984

LOVE EXPRESSED

There is a love that seeks me out,
And calls to me in silent sounds,
And touches deep within the spot
Where hope and promise still abound.
Its pulsing call attracts the mind.
Its touch attunes the human side.
The heartbeat stills, and then I find
That life and spirit there abide.
The soul accepts the offered gift
And in possessing, is possessed,
Through Him, Who offered "All" for all
By "One" Who is the Love expressed.

August, 1983

FED BY THE LIVING WATER

You called to me from the desert of my heart
But I did not recognize You.
Your call reverberated in the hollowness
   of my life,
Like the sound of taut strings caressed
   by the bow.
I followed, drawn by the eerie sounds of love,
And sought You there, in the desert
   of my heart.
And then, You touched me for a love-filled
   moment.
I came upon the source of that love
And discovered that it was a fountain of
   living water.
I bathed there momentarily, thinking that
   I had found all,
And found that the fountain led to a stream.
Drawn by Love, I waded in.
I was smothered by Love —
Lifted and turned and tossed and cleansed.
It was there that I recognized Him for the
   first time,
And I floundered, helplessly, awkwardly,
   longingly,
Towards Him.
Filled with love and longing, I entered
   the stream
Again and again,
To be renewed and stirred, then swept along
Often carried into the rapids and helplessly
   trapped

(Continued)

To be buffeted, sometimes painfully
Then to be strengthened
And buoyed-up by the powerful currents of
   Love,
And carried into warm and peaceful waters
Then left
But not abandoned
There, the Love that had drawn me into
   the stream
Still pulsed within me
Still possessed me
The sounds that had drawn me
Became a melody within
As one would end another would begin
And grow
And fill my heart with Love
To journey with me
Through Life
To Him
Fed by The Living Water
My desert became
A garden of Love

March 19, 1984

EUCHARIST

You Who gave to us Your Body
You Who gave to us Your Blood
Through Your sharing, loving action
Gave Yourself to be our food.

Having been so Graced, I've eaten
Having eaten, been sustained
I have grown dependent on You
When deprived, my hunger pains.

Only "Bread of Life" can feed me
Only You can fill the void
Only if I can receive Thee
Only then my life is buoyed.

For there is naught else to save me
Naught but Thee to strengthen me
Naught but Thy great love to lead me
Only You are life to me.

April 19, 1984

DAILY EUCHARIST

Daily doth the Eucharist feed me
By His ended life resumed
By the Guest that dwells within me
In consuming am consumed.

Present as the blood pulsed through me
Present here within me now
Present in the hope-spring in me
Present His "Eternal" vow.

Oh! The Eucharistic Presence
Is as present now as then
Makes His act of dying "Living"
Shares His Life and Love again.

April 19, 1984

A WHISPERED WORD

However soft a whispered word
If said with love, it can be heard
By one whose heart is "Love" attuned
To sense and sound and touch and wound.

With spirit sensitized by Love,
Words soar with swiftness of a dove
And reach and touch and sear — Inspire
The soul aflame with fervor's fire.

In silent openness and free,
In absence of activity
My love must quietly attune
To One's, Who bears a lover's wounds.

Yes quietly I dwell and wait.
It is not I who choose my fate.
I am in Him and He in me
Oh gracious Love! What joy to "Be."

In patience I must bear and share
Life's jeers and scars and wounds and cares,
To be reminded constantly
Of all the trials You bore for me.

Thy love so burns within my heart
So fires my soul — When we're apart
I pause and listen anxiously —
I must await Your call to me.

Like thunder stirring ground and air,
A whisper tells me You are there.
As lightning's frightening fury chills,
My tremulous heart and soul are thrilled.

(Continued)

39

Your whisper, though a silent sound,
Is strong and clear when love abounds
For quiet though your call may be,
Your silent voice is heard by me.

June 18, 1984

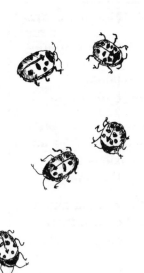

IN SEARCH FOR SELF

In search for self, one can but find,
The inner vineyard's growth entwined.
If all is self, and self is all,
The soul can't grow, and withering falls.
And thrashing there will gasp and groan,
And chill when touched by heart of stone,
For roots from Hell grow midst the vines
To sap the life and taint the wine.

An empty hollowness remains.
A loneliness that gnaws and pains,
A searching, thrashing, grinding quest
For self is naught, without "The Guest."
Alone, deserted, in despair,
Bewildered, hopeless, self laid bare —
The search can lead to "Life" within.
When self is lost, true growth begins.

Enlivened — Drawn by love and light,
The soul will rise, and then take flight
And float on air like winged dove
Caught up in channel of "*Spirited* Love"
Of Son for Father — Father for Son,
Until the soul and "*Spirit*" are one
And carried in that loving swell
Draws strength from "Living Water's" well.

September 16, 1984

MY DESERT PLACE

I'm called to find my desert place,
Throughout the day's tumultuous pace
To solitude, amid the din,
To find a love that waits within.

I close my eyes and there I find
A respite from the worldly grind
From fears and tensions, strife and cares,
Because I find my Saviour there.

I grasp a moment, quiet, but fleet,
And meet within a split heart-beat.
His greeting seems to say to me,
"I've been here long, awaiting thee."

The solitude, though brief and fleeting,
Is poignant with His heavenly greeting.
The fragrance of the moment clings
Through every trial the long day brings.

August 2, 1984

LOVE SPEAKS SOFTLY

Love speaks softly, sometimes whispers
Sometimes joyful, sometimes firm
Always loving, always caring,
So profound, endearing terms.

Just as in the hush of twilight,
When the gentle breeze floats through
Limpid leaves that barely flutter,
If you listen, speak to you.

Intimately, Love's soft whisper
Comes to you at silent times,
When your spirit hears no other
When your heart and soul entwine.

There, within those silent chambers,
Only heart-sounds break the spell
There it is that Love's soft whispers
Pierce the soul, and love waves swell.

Words of comfort pluck your heart strings.
Understanding strains are played.
In the chambers of your "Life-spring,"
Promises of love are made.

Freed, at peace, your soul adores Him,
He, Who is "The Light" — "The Word."
He, Who is "The Source" of true love,
There in silence "All" is heard.

October 18, 1984

YOU ARE THERE

One day You called me. Touched my heart
And warmed the icy chambers there
And melted taut protective shields,
And pierced the walls that made life bare.

You called to me from deep within
Awakened feelings kept at bay
Alerted hope's aggressive strains
To reach for "ONE" to show the way.

So softly, sweetly, You approached
So tenderly, Love's signals swelled
The tiny tendrils slowly crept
Along the conscious sensing cells.

A moment then became an hour.
The hour seemed but a moment long.
The thoughts that played or strayed or stayed
All merged and focused onto "ONE."

But when I looked and You weren't there,
I searched and sought and found life bare.
I longed to feel You close and share
The seeds of love still growing there.

I looked within the shadowed shell
And found unnoticed chinks and flaws,
And fear to leave the known and links
To worldly loves, that lure and draw.

The longing slowly grew and burned
The empty feeling still remained,
I had no gift to offer You.
My heart was dulled. My soul as chained.

(Continued)

46

I searched for ways to make amends
Or recompense to end the breach
That barred me from Your love and You.
I could but love and wait and reach.

You had not left. You waited there.
I'd felt the cleansing of despair.
I'd learned the ways of Light and Love.
Such gifts are Yours alone to share.

You've given all I have to me.
You are the sole redeeming one.
I must abandon all to Thee.
You are the Way. You are the "ONE."

———————————

I am not here. I know not where I am.
Though time is stilled, I'll gladly wait.
For where I am, I know You're there
And You alone control my fate.

January 25, 1985

MOTHER'S TIME

A snow-man can last forever
In the heart of a little girl.
And the time that is spent builds a
   love-monument
Like a sand grain that grows to a pearl.

There is no way to measure the trust or
   the treasure
That grows from the love of the two.
And the other you'd do like a droplet of dew,
Disappears in an ocean-swept view.

For the joy that is shared will always
   be there
In the memory that lives in the two.
And the love-seeds placed there, and the
   faith that is shared,
Make a window to view God's love through.

March 1, 1985

OUTSIDE THE DOOR

I wait for You outside the door
And struggle with the lures and lore
Of worldly wiles that hold me fast,
While measures of my life file past.

So hobbled by the weight of sin
And worldly values deep within,
Yet humbled by the pain and strife,
I fall and fail to grasp at life.

I, crippled, helpless, fail to see
The vision of eternity
That waits within the Temple's folds,
And grasp at goals the world's view holds.

Yet there outside the Temple gate
In bleak despair, I pause and wait
For one to hear my urgent plea,
And offer mite or alms to me.

I search the eyes of passers-by
For rays of hope that there might lie
Within their hearts a tender strain,
To help me through this day of pain.

And then, as if my last, weak cry
Had bridged the void, and I
Though faithless, felt a hope-filled flush,
Through one who turned and sweetly
    touched.

(Continued)

The voice, though firm, enticed and thrilled.
The touch, so tender, heart-beat stilled.
"I have not gold to offer thee,
But what I have, I'll give to thee."

"With what I give, you can be healed."
"Come follow Me, and learn and yield
Your will and offer all you are
To One Who guides the Sun and Star."

I strengthened, lifted by the touch,
Arose, entranced. No longer crushed
By worldly weight of self and sin,
And turned to find new Life within.

The Temple, wherein lies the Life
Became for me a paradise
Of Grace-filled moments leading me
On pathways of Love's Mystery.

And with each touch of love I grew
And learned and then through Grace I knew
That there inside the Temple door,
I'd found the strength I so longed for.

Enthralled by all the grandeur there,
I learned to walk, through loving care,
And though my step may falter now,
The Lord of Life will show me how.

May 1, 1985

HUMILITY

Humility, while nice for some,
Can certainly be overdone,
When those with eyes for piety
Equate it with propriety.
It frightens me how dull I'd be
If I should get humility.
I'm not sure God meant me to be
Too humble, 'cause He gave to me
An overwhelming sense of pride,
A trait that I've heard some deride.
Or could it be that I am dense
And what I have is confidence?
I really don't think that could be,
Because of my humility.
On surface there appears to be
A touch of ambiguity.
If I have any confidence,
It's based in God's omnipotence.
It may be that humility
Is something deep inside of me —
If it appeared too visibly,
I might take pride in what you see.
Let God be God, and me be me,
And in observing, you will see
That what I have to offer God,
Is only what He gave to me.
And so you see, what e'er I do,
I must give credit where it's due.
But I accept with gratitude,
In spite of critic's attitude,
The sense of humor God gave me.
It teaches me humility.

May 24, 1985

52

OH! BLESSED MIST

Oh blessed mist. Oh heavenly dew.
Oh cloud-bank blocking out the view
To hide majestic mountain's grace,
With laden haze that veils its face.

All but a glimpse obscured by thee.
Exciting light-plays — Mystery.
You coyly tease and taunt and thrill
And calm the senses by the still.

But there within that mist-filled sea
Of cloud, resides the entity.
And peaks, though drab or grandly dressed,
must wait there passively and be possessed.

And so, engulfed in limitless mist,
Is reached and touched and bound
    and blessed
Though touching but a drop of dew,
Is intimately joined to all, in You.

July 5, 1985

TO BE WITH YOU

I seek you when the morning dawns.
Awakening, my spirit yawns,
And barely does the thought-stream rise,
When I am calling out to You.

I spend a fleeting moment when
My faltering thoughts escape and then
As if my mind is bound to You,
I have no other thought but You.

I start upon the work I do.
My thoughts keep turning back to You.
A silent word alerts my love.
My heart returns again to You.

I go and come, and go again,
And presently, I don't know when
We've been apart, for constantly,
My soul is drawn to be with You.

July 2, 1985

54

GOD'S TOUCH

God's touch is like a pulsing trill
That darts in deep and thrills the heart.
So sweet, your tremulous soul grows chill —
Held helpless, lest Love's stirrings part.

A searing solace soothes the soul
And holds you powerless in its grasp.
A numbing tenderness enfolds you.
You can't escape. That time has passed.

The paralyzing pleasure pains.
The sweetness penetrates the soul.
A peaceful presence enters in.
The touch is deft and deep and whole.

The soul in silent love is seized.
Enraptured, loved: The soul is changed.
And in the presence of such love
Can only want what God arranged.

July 25, 1985

THE SONG OF SILENCE

A shadow on the ocean floor
Is cast by soaring sea gull wings
That beat a rhythmic pulsing flow,
Accompanying song that silence sings.

The pattern pierces crystal depth,
Accenting sunlight through the sea,
But marks no pathway in the sand —
No trace of touch for one to see.

Its image glides to steady beat,
Unbridled by the powerful purge
Accompanying the silent song
Of swelling water. Mounting surge.

It faithfully, in faultless time
To nature's pulse, is synchronized.
A silent symphony of love
Through Spirit Life, is harmonized.

August 12, 1985

LOVE TIDE

Control my life, Oh Lord of love.
Your will, not mine, be my desire.
Instill in me Thy fervent faith.
Inspire my soul with Spirit's fire.

As Ocean's breadth exceeds my view,
So also does my vision of You.
Magnificence bewilders me.
Tremendous power thrills me through.

Though swelling forces foster fear
And timid faltering shackles me,
Let Wisdom clear my misty sight.
Let Love alone my beacon be.

Lest I fear the darkening depth,
And flee to shore's security,
Accept my weak and wavering faith.
Incite my soul to bravery.

And captured in the surging wake
Of Love-tide's power, Carry me.
And perilous though Love's sea may be,
Let me abandon all to Thee.

October 12, 1985

PRECIOUS MOMENTS

The precious moments near life's close
Are snatched away by fiends, for gold.
Vain promises that life endure,
Distorted hope, Cruel callous cures.
With fear of death and threat of pain,
As tools to twist and trick and drain.
With vision blocked, mind — thought
    obscured,
And pain-wracked body made endure
The endless, prying, preying pain
Of life prolonged, for other's gain.
The love of family, touch of friend,
Cannot be felt as this life ends.
With loved ones barred, no friendly face,
By those who scorn God's will and Grace.
The treasures of these precious hours
Are robbed of dignity and power,
With fearful monsters, tortured cures
Through mankind's ego-manic lures
The life they offer is but death.
True Life in Christ has conquered death.
Love, Faith in God, can help us know
The Joy-filled life to which we go.
Oh God! Please help us to draw near
To You, when promised death prompts fear,
That through Your Grace, in trust, mind free,
We pass through death to "Life" with Thee.

October 18, 1985

OH LOVE!

Oh Love! Awakening with the Dawn,
In concert with the radiant morn,
Arousing me to be reborn.

Oh Love! Aroused, my spirit yearns,
Ignited, touched, it burns
For Your return.

Oh Love! So long unknown to me,
Such depth, intensity,
Exceeds expectancy.

Oh Love! Your touch when all is still,
Thrills when it's just a trill,
To stir my will.

Oh Love! The tender signals sent
Become a sacrament
To spur my soul's ascent.

Oh Love! Time flees, yet time stands still,
Your powerful presence thrills,
Your light instills.

Oh Love! It now is clear to me,
That there can never be
A love more dear to me.

Oh Lord! To know Your love for me,
Love all for love of Thee
Is all You ask of me.

November 15, 1985

KITES

Oh such a brisk and cheerie day!
The sky was bright. The clouds were gay.
They danced about the tree-top rills,
And seem to brush the distant hills.

And grandma, loving kites in flight,
Decided that the day was right
To take the children to a space
Where kites could fly and children race.

That's how it happened, on that day,
When wind and sky came out to play
That grandma had the kites, and knew
That that's what all should go and do.

It's much more normal, I admit,
For grandmas to stay home and knit,
But there are some (perhaps a few),
Who like to do, what children do.

So grandma drove some miles away,
And asked if kids could come and play,
And quick as winks, as children do,
The kids said "Yes!" "We'll fly kites too."

They put on coats and boots and ran,
To grandpa's car, as children can,
And talked of string, and wind, and sky,
And running to get kites to fly.

There never was a better day
For kites to fly, or kids to play.
The day was brisk, the sky was bright:
Excitedly, they launched the kites.

(Continued)

61

They climbed. Climbed high —
   and higher still.
They dipped, and twisted, climbed and fell.
But soon a wind gust aiming high,
Just whisked the kites up in the sky.

And then, a plane came into view
And almost cut the string in two.
It really wasn't very near,
But that's how it appeared from here.

And while we tied and tugged and played,
The chill had crept up on the day.
The cold, soon turned our hands to red.
We shivered as the cool dusk spread.

While those of us, who could, would run
To keep them warm without the sun;
The kites kept climbing up so high,
We each gave winding-in a try.

It ended up with gramp and gram —
One winding, and one pulled by hand.
With everyone both numb and chilled.
The kites came down, and finally stilled.

With brisk wind chilling every bone,
We packed things up and headed home,
Recounting all the tricks and trials
Of flying kites, and Fall wind's wiles.

December 7, 1985

TOUCHED BY LOVE

We seek to know You, with closed mind.
We try to see, but eyes are blind.
We say "I Hear," but ears are blocked.
We say "I'm open," but spirit's locked.

We look and listen, search and seek,
And then ignore You when you speak.
We only want to hear You say
Approving words that grant our way.

But touched by Love, the heart and soul,
Submissive, yields to "Love's" control.
Like windows opened to freshened air,
Our spirit basks in Wisdom, rare.

In silence now, in Your control
We hear with heart and see with soul.
With open mind — Your will, Your view,
Our spirit grows to one with You.

December 8, 1985

LOVE — HATE

We whisper love and shout out hate.
We question, lecture, sneer, debate
The premise of our hate-filled acts,
And feel fulfilled when hate attracts.

We use hate to bring guilt and pain.
We never question what remains —
The Earth or Life or love or hope —
We keep hate's targets in our scope.

Hate sears our soul, and spirit dies.
It sees not rainbow's glow in skies.
It rings in ears and glows in tears,
And weighs souls down towards burning biers.

Hate stifles joy and crowds out life.
It causes all to writhe in strife.
It tears into the heart like nails —
The ignominious self impales.

Hate thrives on hunger, pain, and grief,
And loses sight of Faith's belief.
It wallows in the grime of sin,
And triumphs when the visions dim.

It feeds on devil's dark delights.
It grows on hopelessness and fright.
It gathers others to its fold —
Through trickery, it gains control.

(Continued)

Hate sows in evil, reaps in sin —
And torment tortures Soul within.
The ways of Wisdom fail to grow
In soil sodden by life's blood flow.

But quiet love plods slowly through
The painful barbs that hatred grew.
It suffers with the souls who thrive
On sips of solace in tortured lives.

Hate can't accept the meek — "Poor soul,
With only goodness as its goal,"
With bleak rejection blocking life,
With painful jibes to cause it strife.

Love walks and whispers loving words.
Some hear, but quickly term absurd.
It seeks not self nor wealth nor wins.
It serves its God and stifles sin.

Love stands submissive to the jeers,
And sheds soul-searing, quiet tears.
It waits in Faith, and hopes in Grace,
And lovingly shares life and space.

It uses not its power to show
The futile paths of envy's glow,
But softly, sweetly, humbly, stands
And strives to fit into God's plans.

And whispered love is clearly heard
By One Who is the Way, the Word,
And He, Who is "Love" will reply
To pleas, though but a silent cry.

(Continued)

And one to one, as quiet grows,
The world will seek the "One" who knows,
And in a quiet moment hear
The loving God, Who's always near.

Quite quietly then, the world will feel
The touch of Him, Whose love will heal.
And touched, will open heart and soul,
And know that there is but one goal.

We need not shout nor fear nor hate.
We need not demonstrate, debate.
We need in simple faith to stand
For Christ, Who loves, is in command.

December 27, 1985

WINTER

The cold, black forms of winter rocks,
Their shapes disguised by glazen shocks
Of shimmering ice, reflecting light
In mimicry of fleeting night.

The ice trapped in the brook by storms
Has built up random frozen forms.
The glistening coat's transparent glow
Mirrors the mounds that block the flow.

The cold dark water rushing by
Reflects the cold and threatening sky.
Its depth, like polished pewter-gray
Not yet approached by day-break's rays.

The frigid air, so crisp and cold,
Is whipped by snapping, snarling, bold,
Erratic, wind gusts bending trees,
That twisting, split sharp ice spikes free.

Each footstep meets a sharp reproach.
Frost chatters, as they dare approach.
And shredded grass shrieks under feet
In concert with the rhythmic beat.

And there, beneath the threatening cold
Is life, in rigid, dormant hold —
So mute, in awful, tomb-like still,
Awaiting soundless sign of nature's will.

A message pierces frozen earth
And echoes signals of re-birth
Through flowing brook, and rigid tree,
All sharing nature's mystery.

(Continued)

God speaks through pulsing, silent sounds,
Expressing life, and hope abounds.
Not Spring, nor Summer's brightest day
Has more exciting things to say.

January 19, 1986

OH SILENT SONG

Oh silent song within my breast
That comes along to waken me.
And swelling grows — The love expressed
Assures me that You care for me.

It courses through my soaring soul
Instilling "Spirit's" saving breath
Dispatching life's unworthy goals
Replacing them with Mysteries depth.

The secret sound so soothingly
Expresses life before unknown
And yet, such sweetness can but be
A solace sent by Christ alone.

Oh soothing song, oh saving thrill,
Enveloping, enrapturing me,
To penetrate through senses stilled,
The insights of God's Mystery.

February 10, 1986

THE BREATH OF SPIRIT

I walked along the Ocean's shore,
The children's laughter underscored
The atmosphere that carried me
Lightheartedly towards ecstasy.

I sought out shells amid the stones
And studied patterns blithely honed
By restful flow at water's edge,
A symbol of the power pledged.

I spoke to others, yet I knew
That there within the Ocean's view
Was One Who spoke, unheard by some,
But One Who spoke to everyone.

I stopped and paused and listened well
To silence, bridging sound of swelling
Wave, that broke and rushed ashore,
And then returned to Sea once more.

It wasn't sound or voice I heard,
It wasn't even whispered word —
I felt, I knew, a love expressed.
The tender touch of Spirit's Breath.

It was as if the breeze caressed
My mind, my soul, expressing
Peaceful Presence lovingly,
And drawing ever close to me.

As time went by, each breath I took
Refreshed me, stirred me, bade me look
At all the beauty that surrounds,
And know that in it love abounds.

(Continued)

The time became a prayerful cause
And inwardly I longed to pause,
Surrendering passively to Him,
So sweet the Breath of Love had been.

Though steady, sweet and rhythmic breeze
Kept pace with steps and stops and pleas
Of children's shrill, excited cries —
The Presence never left my side.

I longed to stop time — spend the day,
And bask in Breath of Spirit. Pray
In passive, silent, peaceful calm,
And breathe more deeply, Spirit's balm.

I felt within my pulsing breast
The Spirit's strengthening, saving Breath,
Like cresting water's undertow,
Bestirring soulful, saving flow.

And there, embraced by sea-touched breeze,
With crystal droplets touching me,
The Spirit's Breath instilled in me
The silent peace of ecstasy.

February 26, 1986

FIRST COMMUNION

Today you meet your loving Lord,
and touch Him — Hold Him in your heart
He gives Himself to you as food,
So keep Him close and never part

In Eucharist, Jesus comes to you,
His Body, Soul, Divinity
He wants to share what e'er you do
And stay with you eternally

He'll always be your closest friend
He loves to have you talk to Him
He'll always love you come what may
He'll share His joy and Life within

At quiet times, alone, and still,
You'll know He's there — you're not alone
No matter what you say or do
He'll love you. Make your heart His home.

It's such a special day to be
To know that Jesus lives in you
And waits for you at Mass each day
To share His Life, your whole life through

April 13, 1986

OH GRACIOUS LOVE

Oh gracious Love
Oh saving Grace
Oh beam from Whom
I shade my face
Oh dream
I never dared to dream
Oh cleansing wake
Oh soothing stream
Embracing
Strength-inspiring flow
Of Love
To spur my love to grow
Oh guide me
Chide me
Bid me come
To Thee
When Earth's drear work is done.

May 5, 1986

JOY

Joy reaches out in subtle ways,
And springs from inner-sanctioned rays
Of Spirited growth and saving spark,
And Soul spurred on by Light, through dark.

Inspired senses activate
The will, to stir the action state,
And keyed to "All," enlivens, thrills,
Imparting zeal to do His will.

Absorbed in Love's exciting ways,
Each act becomes a "Power-play,"
Through Him, through Whom all action
    flows,
To share the joyful way to grow.

May 5, 1986

76

SPRING

Oh gentle, sweet, and subtle Spring,
Your color sweet and beckoning,
Expresses in a quiet way
The promised part that Love can play.

The placid colors brushing trees,
And touching tips of flowers' leaves,
And tiny violet temptingly
Betrays life's hidden mystery.

The peaceful rain's percussion pounds
Upon the soul through thrilling sounds,
Awakening inner strength to grow,
Through Grace's unrestricted flow.

And hidden in whites, greens, and browns,
Pigmental power-thrills abound,
And gnarled, fresh, leaf-sprouts spring free,
To be what God meant them to be.

All joyfully are savoring
The silent symphony of Spring
Through cleansing, Sacred, saving signs
Of nature's growth, which God aligns.

May 7, 1986

OH LOVING LORD

Oh loving Lord
Your precious Gifts
Diminish trials
And lift
My soul
From doleful depth
To heights of Grace
Allowing it
To soar in space
Where mystery dwells
And bask
In loving swells
Wherein
The silence saves
Without the need
For word or deed
And there
Absorbed in blessed bliss
I dwell
And all is well
For "Love" is "All"

June 5, 1986

JUDGEMENT

This
Is the God
I feared so long
He waited there
for me to pause
and find Him there
in silent love
and now I burn
for love of Him.
At night I sleepily
awake
and gladly
I forsake
my sleep
to spend the time
with Him
and know His touch
and listen to
His whispered words.
The punishment
I always feared
has faded
almost disappeared.
The punishment
I always feared
is present now
in other's tears
and I
shall suffer
through the years

(Continued)

for others
while my life remains.
Held in His peace
embraced by Love
I fear
not punishment
nor pain
the only thing
that I fear
then
is not to know
that love
again.
I feared
His judgement
now I judge
my deeds
my heart
in light of Love
for
I alone can cause
a breach
and yet, so loved,
can only seek
to serve
surrendering all
to Him
Who lives in me
and I
in Him.

June 6, 1986

UNUTTERED WORDS

Unuttered words may sometimes be
A silent cry — unspoken plea
Or hidden pain or fear or stress
Or something one just can't express.
Or yet, perhaps an unsaid word
May leave a Spirit's word unheard.
But one, if said, might heal or cheer
Through Love's sweet gift God meant
   to share.
Unuttered words raise doubt, cause pain,
Allow a hidden hurt to gain
Or cause despair when view is bleak
Or spur a breach where faith is weak.
A word, if shared, might sometimes spare
Another worry, grief, or care.
But when the love is of God's seed,
The love will patiently await His lead.
And through faith's light will understand
That ail must fit into His plan.

June 6, 1986

THROUGH LOVE

Oh Lord
my love
my hope
my dream
beside Thee
other
seems
to dim
and yet
the beams
of love
You share
envelop
others
in
Your care
and reach
through me
and what
I do
to make of
my love
Your love
too.

June 28, 1986

WHEN WILL WE CARE?

When will we care enough to cry?
We read about the crowds that die
Of fall-out from a tragic fluke,
And casually, we call it "nuke."

The sullen, slow, and painful death
Invades the body, saps the breath —
While selfishness erodes the soul.
It unseen, takes its sinister toll.

Police drag away the one who cares
Enough to flaunt the jeers and stares,
To rise against the silent roar
That subtlely seeps through our door.

It spreads, unseen, throughout the world
And hides in clouds that when unfurled
Spill drops laden with hidden hell,
And slyly waits to maim and kill.

There is no remedy or cure.
Disguised as good, it thrives on lures.
It never stops its spread until
There is no hope, and life is stilled.

The selfish hearts require and will
Their comfort, needs, desires, until
They gratify their greed for gold
And sacrifice their sons and soul.

There is no way to stop its spread.
Released, it reaches all with dread.
The fate of life on Earth is wrought
In seeded sin, and silence bought.

(Continued)

The birth, the life, the grain, and Earth
Is caught up in its creeping girth.
"We need" "We must" "You want"
"Just trust" the greedy power plant will taunt.

"No need to fear the ills it makes —
They'll find a way to make it safe" —
And through our thoughtless, careless gaze
We're trapped within the nuclear haze.

The threat that one, though blind, can see
Has roots in self-idolatry,
By those who feed their ravenous craze
To block guilt for the murderous maze.

Care now, love now, seek now, don't wait
To stop the creeping, heinous fate,
And turn to Him Who loves, and pray
To One Whom Wind and Sea obey.

Then we may care enough to cry, and speak
Of prayer and love, and seek
Our solace in The Power that saves,
And find true peace through Spirit's rays.

July 16, 1986

OH TRUNK OF LIFE

Oh source of strength
Oh trunk of life
so scarred by strain
and gnarled by strife
Tormented
twisted
wounded boughs
accepting meekly
scarring pain
Supporting limbs
that fail to grow
with purpose
met
by cruel distain
You call upon
your stalwart strength
while patiently
you stand and wait
majestic
staunch
enduring all
to draw hope forth
from wrath and hate
You spur life
urge weak limbs
to grow,
through sharing
life-spring's
inner flow
with those that soar

(Continued)

or drift
or run
or burrow
deep within your heart
and daring
each becomes a part
of all you are
and all you do
to ultimately
bide
and live
in You

September 5, 1986

HE SPEAKS TO ME

He speaks to me near wind-swept seas,
And whispers through the gentle breeze,
To touch my soul with Wisdom's ways,
And calm the torment folly plays.

He soothes my mind and stills my soul,
And holds my passions in control.
He clears my vision, guides my thoughts
And mends the breach that turmoils'
   wrought.

He guides me through trials, pain,
   and wrath,
Surmounting pitfalls in the path
That leads towards goals, thought fantasy —
Unreachable to such as me.

The trials of hazards, doubts, and fears,
Accompanied by rebuffs and jeers,
Are smoothed by gentle touch and word,
In peaceful pauses — Silence heard.

Though darkness dims my spirit's sight,
The Grace of Faith reveals the light,
Allowing "Hope-springs" view to grow,
To lead me on towards Life's Love flow.

And in the pause's Mystic still,
Are whispered words of Wisdom's will,
And confidence in path to trod,
Illumined by the Grace of God.

July 28, 1986

IT'S NOT MY WORLD

It's not "my" world
that's crumbling
It's not "my" puppet
Not "my" string
I only think
I'm in control
It's not "my" love
that stirs "my" soul
I felt the threat
of pain and death
and wrestled with
a labored breath
in morbid fear
I called to You
I searched within
and then I knew
Your Grace permits
each thing I do
Yes, all I have
is "gift" from You.

September 16, 1986

AWAKEN FROM YOUR SLEEP

Arise! Awaken from your restless sleep.
You need no longer seek out peace
In safe cocoon, or flee in blind retreat —
For I am here to bear with you
The cares that pierce your heart.

Break from the pattern of your mold
And follow paths that I have hewn
And told you of,
For I was where you are,
And even then, you followed Me.

No evil may enter when I am so near.
And if you falter, listen and hear
The words of comfort I will share.
And there within your heart,
You'll gather strength to bear.

Fear not! My Grace will light your way.
At peace, accept the trials and strife,
And in serenity, receive my strength.
And walking in my Grace
Reflect My Life.

December 8, 1986

WITHIN MY REACH

If heaven lies within my reach,
It rests within my soul, and speaks
In silent, tender ardent strains
To summon me to Love's embrace.

The subtle surge, so strong, yet sweet,
Instills a message — Sure — Complete.
Revealing such a luring goal —
A gentle Lord to soothe my soul.

It shows me daring dreams to dream,
And lifts me, lightly, through a stream
Of surging, swelling, misty, still —
Enlightening mind and soul and will.

There reason rests and senses sing,
And knowledge knows no offering,
While time serenely passes masked in mist.
And stillness touches, tender as a kiss.

The saving love-seeds Grace will sow,
Will hide within my heart to grow —
Love's presence reigns and peace exists,
There, in the heavenly blessedness of bliss.

December 25, 1986

92

I AM NOT
"OLD" OR "ELDERLY"

I am not "old" or "elderly"
I am not "senior"
I am me!
The same "me" I have always been
I'm me!

I don't want more
I don't need less
'Though sometimes, now, I must confess
I'm slower, some, at certain things
But still, I'm me!

You may not always think I'm right
But I'd really like the right to think
The way I wish, and in my time,
So I can keep my own life line
And be, just me!

I don't believe in certain things
But what I think affects the things
I do, and say, and feel, and see —
The simple fact of life is that
I'm me!

I'm not statistics! Not an age! —
Correct proportions on a page
Nor measured like an entity
But vary, as I grow to be
Just me!

Don't try to see inside my mind
Or judge my deeds or you will find

(Continued)

It baffles you because I'm me
Not you, or someone else — I am myself
I'm me!

I try to learn the will of God,
And 'though some sometimes think I'm odd,
I use the will that God gave me
To do His will and try to still
Be me!

There have been times when I've been
    wrong,
And life has not been all a "song,"
But as I've made my way along,
I've always tried to change, and still
Be me!

I still have pride. Inside I know
That time has made me wiser — grow
Through "Ins" and "Outs" and "Ups"
    and "Downs"
To recognize my faults and gifts,
And yet, Be me!

I now accept my trials and woes,
But 'though I falter some, I know
That I can learn through love and grow
In Wisdom's ways, and still
Be me!

I've also learned
That love is all
And 'though I'm wiser, I can fall,
And fail to love, and learn some more,
And still Be me!

(Continued)

I won't be condescended to,
I still would like to do for me
Whatever I am able to.
To live out all my life-time through
As me!

I must admit, with some chagrin,
I sometimes find the shape I'm in
Is not as great as it "could be," but I'd
    appreciate
It if you, whenever I come into view,
Would still see me!

I thank you, and appreciate
Your kindness, and I think it's great
When lovingly you help me out
When I am feeling "down" and doubt my
    ability
To be me!

As long as when you look at me,
No matter what my age may be,
And see that strong, weak, bent, or straight,
You still can see and lovingly refer to me
As me!

So firmly I reiterate
That though my age is growing "great"
That I refuse to separate
The "me" I'm now and used to be —
I'm me!

And when I reach the very end
And have no time to share or spend,
I hope that God will like the me
That He has tried to make of me,
And still love me!

January 5, 1987

GOD'S LOVE

God's love, like God,
can't be described
in human terms,
through human eyes
Yet love is such
a subtle thing
escaping barriers
limiting its reach
that cleverly
its touch can stretch
beyond Devine
and meet
the one beloved.
Unlimited
by mind
or myth
Love seeps inside
to sweetly kiss
and stir
and thrill
with unknown gifts
Unknown
yet known
in some uncanny way
or sense
by one who loves.
Soul soothed, and knowing
stilled
is stirred.
It seeks no other
recompence.

(Continued)

Soul wants no other
hears no sound
so loved is one
who Love has found.
There, pride is quashed
temptation tossed
and sin is washed away.
The soul is bared
and seared
and cleansed
Love sows
and kneads
and knits
and mends
while silently
its signal sends.
Now spent
the empty soul is held
and filled with longing
urgent
fierce
Is drawn to merge
and meld
and mesh.
And welded fast
by Spirit's spark
is deeply
pierced
with need
then freed
enlightened by the glow.
Then sanguine seeds of Love
are sown

(Continued)

and nourished
by the strong Grace flow
Light beams are shed
and power spread
sublimely
sweetly
Soul is stretched
and fed
and filled with peace
and swelled with love
and in the stillness
Soul has grown.
God's Love is known.

January 15, 1987

YOUR CALL

Why is it Lord,
when You reach out
to touch us,
we just turn about
and rush off
in another way
afraid of words
that You might say,
to draw us
ever closer —
near,
we run away
and hide
in fear?
For love requires
sacrifice:
Less won't suffice
and our response
and discipline
allowing You
to reach within.
But once we feel
that touch
inside
unable now
to run
and hide
We stop and look
and know it's You
and there is
nothing else to do

(Continued)

but wait
be still
be in Your peace
and listen passively
to each
resounding call:
For love
demands love in return
and love
can lead a heart to yearn
for You
and lift Your Cross
and climb
and die to sin
and then
You enter in.
And in the space
prepared within,
You share Your love
and then
your loving ways
entice
and thrill
until You fill
the Soul with Grace
and in the place
prepared
You share Your life
there to remain
within,
to touch the heart
and You become a part
of all we think

(Continued)

and say
and do.
So loved
we can't resist
a call
to be
with You.

February 8, 1987

OH LORD!

Oh Lord!
You made the World so joyful, bright
Its Moon reflects the Sunshine's light
Its rolling hills reach constantly,
To stretch towards mountain's majesty.
There trees of every shape and hue
Lift bough and branch in praise of You.
And flower and bush excite the eye
And tall grass waves as breeze floats by.
While flowing streams rush swiftly through
To join the Ocean's endless view.
And busy birds fly gracefully
To carry song from tree to tree —
While cooing doves absorb the Sun
And share their peace with everyone.
Where creatures great and creatures small
Share their great gifts of joy with all.
And mankind graced with will and wit
Can gain Life through Your Own Spirit.
Through loving touch and mystic thrills
You share Your Wisdom, show Your Will.
Then lured by Love are drawn within
To find our source of origin.
There signs of love are everywhere
And grand Grace gardens glisten there,
And love seeds stirred by subtle sounds
Begin to grow as Grace surrounds
To fill the space with fragrance, sweet,
Replete with Joy, Love, Life — Complete.
While silent sounds speak ardent words,
And all is peace when Love is heard.

February 15, 1987

LORD, TEACH ME!

Teach me of Your Love, Oh Lord!
Speak to me and stir my soul.
Teach me daring dreams to dream
How to make my life more whole.
Teach me to call out to You,
Trust You, Let You lead me too.
Teach Faith when fear blocks my view,
Making me withdraw from You.
Teach me how to find my way
Through the folly doubt can play.
Teach me how to know Your will,
How to make my stirred mind still.
Teach me to seek You alone,
How to make my heart Your home.

February 20, 1987

ECHOES OF SILENCE
by Helen Hayes Veitch

INDEX

LIST OF ILLUSTRATIONS